THE MAKING OF AN INSURANCE WARRIOR

Over 500 Need to Ask Insurance Questions

Keith Kauten

authorHOUSE®

AuthorHouse™
1663 Liberty Drive
Bloomington, IN 47403
www.authorhouse.com
Phone: 1-800-839-8640

First published by AuthorHouse 8/26/2010

ISBN: 978-1-4520-6781-0 (e)
ISBN: 978-1-4520-6780-3 (sc)

Library of Congress Control Number: 2010911887

Printed in the United States of America

This book is printed on acid-free paper.

Contents

About the Author

The experiences as a farm boy growing up in northern Iowa along with loving and devout parents helped to mold me into who I am today. As a small token of my appreciation for all their years of hard work and dedication through good times and bad I would like to dedicate this book to them.

My life began February 24, 1960, in rural farming community in northern Iowa. That year I have been told was a hard winter year with massive amounts of snow. The things that come to my mind as I went through the early years of my life where how dedicated my parents were to the farming career. Most all breakfast, lunch, and dinner conversations consisted of serious talk of the economics of farming, both good and bad. As I look back on the early years in northern Iowa, I have to say I am thankful to have gone through those years. My parent's *dedication*, *persistence*, and *hard work* rubbed off on me as I made it through my adolescent and early adulthood years.

The *dedication, persistence,* and *hard work* that my parents had during my early years have been a business and personal model used in my everyday life since then. I have seen many rewards from *dedication, persistence,* and *hard work* beginning with my graduation from high school in 1978. Next came graduation from an area community college with a degree in auto body and painting in 1979. Finally, the most gratifying was graduation from Drake University with a four-year business degree in insurance and finance in 1993.

That *dedication, persistence,* and *hard work* that I was taught at an early age in northern Iowa by two modest, hardworking people—my parents—is still part of my life today. The last twenty years of my life have been focused on building an insurance agency in my local community of Bettendorf, Iowa: Keith Kauten Insurance Agency Inc. To all of you that allowed me the opportunity to be your insurance agent, I say thank you with a sincere, heartfelt thanks.

To: Ken and Lenora, Ernie and Carol, Mary, Zachary, Peter, Melissa,

Leah, Sarah, Deb, Diane, Denise, all significant others, grandkids, nieces, nephews, and all other family members, I love you.

Why This Book

My sincere and heartfelt motivation for writing this book has risen out of and because of the stressful economic conditions facing individuals and families of today. The last twenty years of my life have been devoted to serving clients as their insurance agent. I have worked to match needs and wants with the financial budgets that were before us and available at the time. However, I have come to realize and witness that the industry I love, worked in, and was educated in is one of many industries that are causing economic stress in the family today.

The vision I have for this book is to help equip you as a consumer before purchasing any and all types of insurance. I don't intend to make you an expert, but I do intend on sharing with you the knowledge I have gained over the last twenty-four years. My intention for the book is to be an easy read with thought-provoking questions. I have included the questions for the purpose of helping you ask the right questions. When purchasing insurance, you have to ask questions and not feel like the questions you are asking are dumb or do not apply. Further, my vision for the book is that it will help consumers young and old be confident when making their insurance purchases.

Also, I have shared some hypothetical situations that are simple, to the point, and in some case real life. Further, I hope the book will convey a real-life message to readers before something actually happens to them. Hopefully this book might create a picture in their minds that could save their lives or save them time and money.

You as a consumer are purchasing an intangible product when you buy insurance. Insurance is a product that cannot be touched or seen. Another goal for this book is to give the consumer some tangible information to make the right decisions when purchasing insurance from their local insurance agent or buying online from someone he or she does not know and cannot see. Most importantly, my intentions for the book are to help the insurance consumer be most informed and knowledgeable, for knowledge is power.

Auto:

Asking

the Right

Questions?

❏ Who is covered insured under my auto policy?

❏ Who is the named insured under my auto policy?

❏ Will I get temporary identification cards?

❏ How many days should I expect it to take before the policy and the original identification cards come in the mail?

❏ Is e-mail an option for receiving identification cards?

❏ What type of vehicle is covered under my auto policy?

❏ What does bodily injury (BI) liability coverage actually cover?

❏ What does property damage (PD) coverage actually cover?

❏ What is the maximum bodily injury amount paid out with split limits?

❏ What is the maximum bodily injury amount paid out with single limits?

❏ What is the difference between split-limit liability and single-limit liability?

❏ Is there an implied deductible on liability coverage?

❏ Is there a deductible applied on medical expense coverage?

❏ How are my rates determined?

❏ Is there a credit scoring system to determine my premium?

❏ I have liability on my vehicles. Will I get any help from the insurance company when I have a not-at-fault accident with someone who has no insurance?

❑ If I cancel my policy, will it be a prorated cancellation or short-rate cancellation?

❑ Do I need to mention customized parts?

❑ Will customized parts be included in a claim?

❑ What is the subrogation process of my auto policy?

❑ What does betterment mean?

❑ Will a new engine in my old vehicle help for a better claim settlement in the event of a total loss?

❑ How many claims can I submit before I get cancelled?

❑ Can anyone drive my vehicle?

❑ Does my vehicle have to be titled in my name to insure it under my policy?

❑ When does my policy go into effect?

❑ What is the maximum property damage paid out with split limits for a property damage claim?

❑ What is the maximum property damage paid out with single limits for a property damage claim?

❑ How many vehicles can be on one policy?

❑ Will your company be open on Saturday and Sunday with a call center?

❑ Is monthly payment EFT available?

❑ Can I pay with my credit card?

❑ Is monthly payment mail delivery available?

- ❏ Is it cheaper if I pay in full?

- ❏ Are late charges assessed?

- ❏ Which payment method is cheaper?

- ❏ Will speeding tickets on my record affect my insurance rates?

- ❏ How will a DUI or OWI affect my insurance?

- ❏ Will I need to add my kids to the policy when they become sixteen?

- ❏ Will I need to add my kids who have school permits to my auto policy?

- ❏ What is the minimum coverage required by my residence state law?

- ❏ At what point should my vehicle be listed as an antique or classic?

- ❏ If I lock my keys in my vehicle will there be coverage to call a locksmith to unlock the doors?

- ❏ Do I have immediate coverage when I replace a car?

- ❏ Can I insure a motorcycle on my auto policy?

- ❏ How do I get my towing bill paid?

- ❏ Can I cancel my auto policy without being penalized?

- ❏ When I have an accident, whom should I call?

- ❏ When I move to another state, does my insurance transfer?

- ❏ When I carry personal belongings in my vehicle, does auto or homeowners insurance provide coverage?

- ❏ Do you plan on staying an agent with this company?

❑ Is your company doing anything to reduce the cost of insurance to consumers?

❑ Will I get a multi-vehicle discount?

❑ Will I get a multi-policy discount?

❑ What are the different discounts available to save money?

❑ Will driving more or fewer miles affect the premiums?

❑ If a driver is in the military, away from home, or out of the country, can insurance be suspended?

❑ Can a vehicle be put in storage when not driven?

❑ If I am pulling a trailer behind a covered auto and it comes unhooked and is destroyed, will it be covered?

❑ If I'm pulling a trailer and it hits another vehicle, will I have liability coverage?

❑ What is your company's AM Best rating?

❑ When will my rates go down after an accident?

❑ At what age do rates start to come down?

❑ When I get married, will auto insurance be cheaper than when I am single?

❑ When was the last time your insurance company had a rate decrease?

❑ Would I be at-fault if I hit someone who was backing out of a parking spot the same time I was?

❑ What happens if damages are over the coverage limits?

❑ How many days do I have before my policy will lapse for nonpayment?

❑ How many payment options does the insurance company have available?

❑ How long after an accident do I have to turn in an auto claim?

❑ Will I get surcharged for an at-fault collision accident?

❑ Will I get surcharged for a comprehensive claim?

❑ Will I get surcharged for a not-at-fault accident?

❑ How many years will I get surcharged for an accident?

❑ Do I need vehicle identification numbers at application time?

❑ Am I responsible to get the bank loan information to the insurance company?

❑ Are CDs covered under the auto policy if stolen out of my vehicle?

❑ Is my cell phone covered if stolen out of my vehicle?

❑ Will I have coverage under my policy for water damage?

❑ What happens if I seriously injure someone or kill him or her in an accident?

❑ Where should I have the vehicle towed when I can't drive from an accident?

❑ When can I add my future wife or husband to my policy?

❑ My vehicles have liability-only coverage. Does the insurance company have any responsibility to me?

❑ Do I need a current driver's license from the state in which I live to purchase insurance on my vehicle?

❑ Can I pay with a credit card over the phone?

❑ Will coverage go into effect on my new vehicle via voice mail?

❑ Can I insure a motor home on my auto policy?

❑ Can I insure a trailer on my auto policy?

❑ Can I insure a horse trailer on my auto policy?

❑ What type of state do we live in (i.e., medical income protection or personal injury protection)?

❑ What is the minimum medical limit available?

❑ What is the maximum medical limit allowed?

❑ Is medical coverage first dollar (i.e., will the insurance company pay first)?

❑ How will the premiums differ from the lowest to highest coverage?

❑ Where should medical bills be sent as I get them?

❑ Will medical coverage provide coverage to passengers in my car?

❑ Will my policy cover lost wages?

❑ Does the company have higher deductibles available?

❑ Is the insurance company more concerned with severity of claims or frequency of claims?

❑ How does a comprehensive claim compare to a collision claim with regards to rates going up?

❏ How many collision claims can I submit before I'm cancelled?

❏ How many comprehensive claims can I submit before I'm cancelled?

❏ How does repairing glass vs. replacing glass differ with regards to cost savings?

❏ Is there an air-bag discount?

❏ Is there a multi-vehicle discount?

❏ Is there a good-student discount?

❏ What classifies you as a good student?

❏ Do you have an anti-lock-brake discount?

❏ Do you have good-driver discounts?

❏ Do you have empty-nest discounts?

❏ How old of a vehicle can still have comprehensive and collision coverage?

❏ When should I drop comprehensive and collision coverage and go with just liability?

❏ Can I have comprehensive coverage without collision coverage?

❏ Can I have someone on my auto policy who is not family?

❏ Can I drive someone's car as long as I get permission without being on his or her policy?

❏ Will there ever be a situation in which I will receive a brand new car after mine is totaled?

❏ Under what circumstances will my windshield be repaired vs. replaced?

❑ If an animal gets in my car and destroys the interior, do I have coverage?

❑ Are there any times where the deductibles are waved?

❑ If my car goes in the garage for mechanical repairs, will my rental coverage pay for the rental?

❑ How often do insurance companies check motor vehicle records?

❑ Does uninsured motorist (UIM) cover the vehicle or my bodily injuries?

❑ Does underinsured motorist (UNIM) cover the vehicle or my bodily injuries?

❑ What minimum limits are available?

❑ What maximum limits are available?

❑ Can I decline uninsured motorist (UIM) and underinsured motorist (UNIM) coverage?

❑ Can I file a claim for bodily injuries if the other driver has no insurance or is underinsured?

❑ Will filing a claim under uninsured or underinsured motorist coverage raise my rates?

❑ How many towing claims are allowed per policy period?

❑ Does towing cover me if I lock my keys in the car?

❑ Will I ever lose my privilege to have towing?

❑ Will towing coverage pay to start my car in the winter if it is stalled?

❑ Will towing pay for the battery if I need it to be replaced?

❑ How do I get reimbursed for my bills?

❑ Does it matter how old the car is when asking for towing?

❑ What are the minimum and maximum towing limits available?

❑ Do I need to call the insurance company before my vehicle is towed?

❑ Do I pick the rental company from which I will purchase a rental car?

❑ Does rental coverage only apply when an accident occurs?

❑ What does it typically cost to rent a vehicle similar to what I'm driving?

❑ How many days after an accident can I expect to get a rental vehicle?

❑ Does my coverage extend over to a rented vehicle?

❑ What happens if I wreck the rental vehicle?

❑ Can I get a rental vehicle from my policy if the accident is not my fault?

❑ Will I be able to use my rental coverage anytime?

❑ Will I have the same coverage on the rental as I have on my own vehicle?

❑ Will I ever lose the privilege to have rental vehicle coverage?

❑ What will happen if I wreck my vehicle and then wreck a rental vehicle?

❑ I'm a newly licensed driver. When will my rates go down?

❑ Will you send proof of insurance to my bank?

❑ Will the bank get a copy of the insurance at renewal?

❑ Do I need the loan number on my policy?

❑ Are there additional coverages that I need to know about?

❑ How many consecutive months do I have to carry insurance before I can get a better rate?

❑ I have a rock chip in my windshield. Can it be fixed?

❑ If my windshield is chipped and repaired, will my deductible be waived?

❑ Will I have coverage for extra expenses if I am in an accident out of town?

❑ Are personal belongings, such as clothes, in my car covered under my auto policy?

❑ Under what area of my insurance policy is fire damage covered?

❑ Is vandalism covered under my auto insurance policy?

❑ Can I purchase a non-owner auto policy?

❑ Can I purchase an insurance policy without owning a car?

❑ Do I have a grace period at the end of my policy period?

❑ If moving from state to state, how long do I have to change my insurance?

❑ Will a higher deductible lower my premiums?

❑ If I have a limb severed in an accident, do I have any coverage?

❑ If I'm killed in an accident, will my family have coverage other than a life insurance policy?

❑ If I'm disabled in an accident, do I have disability insurance?

❑ If my pet is killed while riding in my vehicle, do I have coverage for the pet?

❑ While driving my vehicle for company errands, am I covered?

❑ How do I get my name on the identification cards?

❑ Define the first named insured?

❑ Is there a discount for being a safe driver?

❑ Who is responsible for setting up a rental vehicle?

❑ Explain when negligence comes into play?

❑ How many estimates do you require from me on my damaged vehicle?

❑ What is considered roadside assistance?

❑ What limits of coverage do I have for roadside assistance?

❑ Are acts of terrorism a covered loss under my auto policy?

❑ Can I insure my company business vehicle on my personal auto policy?

❑ Can I insure a camper trailer on my auto policy?

❑ Can I insure a motor home on my personal auto policy?

❑ How many months do I have to turn in a claim?

❑ Should I immediately call in a claim to the claim office?

❑ What rental car company do I have to go through?

❑ Does the insurance company have a specific rental company it uses?

Home:
Asking
the Right
Questions?

❑ Is my homeowners insurance premium determined by credit scoring?

❑ Do I have an all-risk policy or named-peril policy?

❑ Will you explain the difference between all-risk and named peril?

❑ Will I have a replacement cost policy or actual cash value policy (ACV) policy?

❑ Will this policy have an inflation guard built in each year?

❑ Does my policy have an additional amount of insurance provision for dwelling coverage?

❑ Will flood damage be covered under my home policy?

❑ If I'm on the golf course and my golf clubs are stolen, are they covered?

❑ Will water seepage from runoff water be covered under my policy?

❑ What is my earthquake deductible?

❑ Would damage caused by a power surge be covered?

❑ What is my mine-subsidence deductible?

❑ Do I need earthquake coverage?

❑ Do I need mine-subsidence coverage?

❑ Will I be covered if my horse breaks out of its pen and runs into the path of an oncoming vehicle?

❑ Do I need a rider for jewelry coverage?

❑ Do I need a rider for guns?

❑ Are there other things I need to schedule or for which I need to have a rider?

❑ How many claims can I submit before I get cancelled?

❑ Does insurance cover anything buried under the ground (e.g., a well, plumbing from the house to the street)?

❑ Will my entire roof be replaced if I have hail damage?

❑ How much mold coverage do I have on my policy?

❑ Will I be reinstated if my policy lapses for non-payment?

❑ How many days do I have to make my payment before I get a late payment or cancellation notice?

❑ Can I have a wood stove in my house?

❑ Does it cost extra to have a wood stove or fireplace in my house?

❑ What coverage is available that is not currently on my policy?

❑ When I have a fire and can't live in my house, will I have loss of use coverage?

❑ Will medical expense coverage take care of my medical needs?

❑ Will medical expense coverage take care of an injured guest on my property?

❑ Will I need to contact the insurance company when I move to a new house at a new location?

❑ Will my furniture be covered in a moving van I rent?

❑ Will my furniture be covered in a moving van my company purchases to move my things?

❑ If I'm not closing for a month at a new house, will my furniture be covered in a storage shed or company warehouse?

❑ Does the insurance company require me to have an itemized list of all contents being claimed?

❑ What home deductibles are available?

❑ Are there separate wind and hail deductibles?

❑ What is the minimum deductible available?

❑ What is the maximum deductible available?

❑ Do swimming pools increase the cost of insurance?

❑ Do trampolines increase the cost of insurance?

❑ Can the liability from my home policy extend to my rental properties?

❑ Is it cheaper to extend liability coverage from my homeowners policy to a rental property than to have a separate policy?

❑ Can I insure my boat on my home policy?

❑ Is it cheaper to insure my boat on my homeowners policy than on a separate policy?

❑ Is a sump pump covered?

❑ Is sewer backup coverage offered automatically?

❑ What limits are available with sump pump and sewer backup?

❑ Will sump pump and sewer backup coverage have a separate deductible?

- ❑ Will animals ever be covered on the policy (and if so, to what amount)?

- ❑ Will trees ever be covered on the policy (and if so, to what amount)?

- ❑ Should I take video photos of my personal possessions?

- ❑ Do I need to cancel my current policy before my new policy goes into effect?

- ❑ Are there discounts for burglar alarm systems?

- ❑ Are computers covered for family members away at college or school?

- ❑ Are personal property items of a student covered when away at school?

- ❑ What limits will personal property and computers be covered for?

- ❑ Is it my responsibility to call my bank when changing insurance companies?

- ❑ If a claim occurs and checks are written, will checks be made out to the bank and me?

- ❑ If my cell phone is stolen, will it be covered by my home policy?

- ❑ If my mortgage company fails to make a timely payment and my policy lapses, can I reinstate?

- ❑ Is mysterious disappearance a covered cause of loss as part of the basic homeowners policy?

- ❑ Is fire a covered cause of loss under my homeowners insurance?

- ❑ Is lighting a covered cause of loss under my homeowners insurance?

- ❑ Is windstorm a covered cause of loss under my homeowners insurance?

❑ Is hail damage a covered cause of loss under my homeowners insurance?

❑ What is a peril as it relates to insurance?

❑ I live in a condominium, what type of insurance do I need?

❑ Do I need special coverage for the swing set in my backyard?

❑ Do I need a fence around my property if I have a swimming pool?

❑ If my bikes are stolen out of the garage, are they covered?

❑ Will my hearing aids be covered if the dog eats them?

❑ Is there a discount for dead bolts on my doors?

❑ Is there a discount for smoke detectors?

❑ Is there a discount for fire extinguishers?

❑ If my keys are lost or stolen, do I have coverage to change the locks?

❑ Do I have coverage when my piano students are at my house practicing?

❑ Is an all-risk policy better then a named-peril policy?

❑ Is it true that for every loss, there has to be a cause of loss?

❑ How is personal property coverage determined on my home policy?

❑ How is loss of use or additional living expense (ALE) determined?

❑ Do I have coverage on a brick retaining wall in my backyard?

❑ Are fences covered as other structures?

❑ Are fences covered as part of the dwelling?

- ❑ How is replacement cost calculated on my house?

- ❑ Should paintings or fine arts be covered on a rider?

- ❑ Is cash money covered if stolen?

- ❑ What dogs will the insurance company accept?

- ❑ What dogs will the insurance company not accept?

- ❑ Will the insurance company accept exotic animals?

- ❑ Should I make a video of all my personal possessions?

- ❑ If I make a video of my personal possessions, should I keep a copy off-premise and give a copy to the insurance company?

- ❑ Would you give me an example of a cause of loss?

- ❑ Should I make an itemized list of all my personal contents?

- ❑ What cost-saving discounts are available?

- ❑ If my identity is stolen, do I have identity theft coverage?

- ❑ If my pet is killed in a fire, do I have coverage to replace it?

- ❑ I have several buildings not attached to my house. Are they covered?

- ❑ Will I have liability coverage if my horse gets loose and causes an accident?

- ❑ Are my children's bikes automatically covered under the policy?

- ❑ Should bikes be scheduled items?

- ❑ Are bikes covered for all-risk or named-peril coverage?

- ❑ Is a cracked picture window covered under my insurance policy?

❏ What does it really mean to have replacement-cost coverage?

❏ Is there a difference between guaranteed replacement and replacement?

❏ Is there a discount for having a burglar alarm?

❏ Is there a discount for being claim-free?

❏ Do I have any responsibility after a claim?

❏ Do I have coverage on my child's musical instrument away from home?

❏ How do I make sure I have mysterious disappearance coverage?

❏ What coverages do I have for my above-ground pool / in-ground pool?

❏ Are my furs covered under my homeowners policy?

❏ Would I have better coverage if I schedule my furs?

❏ Should I have people doing work on my house show proof of insurance?

❏ Explain the subrogation process for my homeowners policy.

❏ Is there a replacement-cost formula for insuring my home?

❏ What is considered personal property coverage?

❏ What is considered an other structure?

❏ Is mold a covered cause of loss under my homeowners policy?

❏ What are the limits of coverage for mold under my policy?

❑ If I cancel my homeowners policy, will I get a prorated or short-rate refund?

❑ If an earthquake tremor causes my foundation to crack, am I covered?

❑ Should computers be scheduled or have a rider?

❑ When would trees be covered under my homeowners insurance policy?

❑ Are antiques automatically covered under my homeowners insurance?

❑ Are collectibles automatically covered under my homeowners insurance?

❑ If my house is infested with bats, is there coverage for their removal?

❑ If my child hurts another child, do I have liability insurance coverage?

❑ Do I have lock replacement coverage if my keys are stolen?

❑ Will having a home security system save on insurance costs?

❑ If my house is damaged during a riot, am I covered?

❑ Are books covered automatically under my insurance policy?

❑ Should books be covered under a named-peril or all-risk policy?

❑ Should paintings be covered under a named-peril or all-risk policy?

❑ At what point is a house said to be not repairable and replaced with a new house?

❑ Do I have coverage for the removal of my damaged house?

❑ Is my home-based business covered under my homeowners policy?

❑ Is any business equipment covered under my homeowners policy?

❑ Can I work on cars in my garage?

❑ Are animals covered anytime under my homeowners policy?

❑ If someone sued me today, what is the maximum protection I would have to protect my family?

❑ Would you explain depreciation holdback?

❑ Is inventory for my home business covered under my homeowners policy?

❑ What is the fire rating of the responding fire department to my house?

❑ When depreciation is held back, what documents are needed to get the final settlement?

Renters:

Asking

the Right

Questions?

❑ Can I purchase a replacement cost policy?

❑ Can I purchase an actual cash value (ACV) policy?

❑ Which policy, ACV or replacement, gives me better coverage?

❑ What are the minimum limits of coverage for a replacement cost policy?

❑ What are the maximum limits of coverage for a replacement cost policy?

❑ What are the maximum limits of coverage for an actual cash value policy?

❑ What are the minimum limits of coverage for an actual cash value policy?

❑ Will the insurance company automatically send a certificate of coverage to my leasing company?

❑ Are my waterbed and the damage it causes covered?

❑ Are my personal belongings covered worldwide under my renter's policy?

❑ Should I make a video of all my personal possessions?

❑ Should I make an itemized list of all my personal possessions?

❑ What are my limits of coverage?

❑ Do I have liability and medical expense coverage under my renter's policy?

❑ Do I need to schedule anything on my renter's policy?

❑ Can jewelry be scheduled on my renter's policy?

❑ Are my personal belongings covered when in a storage unit?

❑ What deductible do I have on my policy?

❑ What deductibles are available?

❑ If I move out of one apartment or house to another, should I contact the insurance company?

❑ If someone slips and falls outside of my apartment, am I responsible for his or her injury?

❑ If someone slips and falls inside my apartment, am I responsible for his or her injury?

❑ If I start a fire accidentally and cause damage to other apartments, what is my degree of responsibility?

❑ If I store some of my personal contents away from my apartment, is there coverage?

❑ Is cash covered under my renter's policy?

❑ Are dogs covered under a renter's policy?

❑ Are exotic pets covered under my renter's policy?

❑ How many claims can I have before I get cancelled?

❑ Should I have fire extinguishers in my apartment?

❑ Can I take out a renter's policy for my son or daughter while he or she is away at school?

❑ Do I need to take a renter's policy out for my son or daughter while he or she is away at school?

❑ Do I have coverage under my homeowners policy to cover my son or daughter's personal things while he or she is away at school?

❑ What does covered territory mean?

Motorcycle: Asking the Right Questions?

❑ Will my motorcycle be covered on my auto or homeowners policy?

❑ Can I insure more than one motorcycle on the same policy?

❑ Should a four-wheel ATV have a policy of its own?

❑ Is my motorcycle helmet covered when I have an accident?

❑ Do you give a discount to clients who have taken a safety course?

❑ If my motorcycle breaks down out on the road, do I have coverage?

❑ Will I have to include all drivers in the household on my motorcycle policy?

❑ Are clothes in my saddlebags covered?

❑ Will the leather gear I wear be covered?

❑ Does my policy offer me rental coverage?

❑ Do you insure scooters licensed for the road?

❑ Do you insure three-wheeled motorcycles?

❑ Do you insure homemade motorcycles?

❑ Will my motorcycle be insured at replacement cost or actual cash value (ACV)?

❑ Will saddlebags, the windshield, extra chrome, and custom paint be covered?

❑ What deductible limits can I carry on my motorcycle?

❑ Will my coverage be suspended during the winter months?

❑ Can I carry comprehensive coverage without collision coverage?

- ❑ Can I carry collision coverage without comprehensive coverage?

- ❑ If I take my motorcycle to the drag strip once a month, am I covered?

- ❑ If I buy a new motorcycle on Saturday and trade my old one in, is the new one covered immediately?

- ❑ What are the minimum limits of liability I can carry?

- ❑ What are the maximum limits of liability I can carry?

- ❑ Can I let my friends use my motorcycle without putting them on the policy?

- ❑ If my motorcycle has a flat out on the highway, do I have roadside coverage?

- ❑ If I trailer my motorcycle, how will it be covered?

- ❑ Does the motorcycle have to be titled in my name before I insure it?

- ❑ Will speeding tickets increase the cost of my motorcycle insurance?

- ❑ When is a motorcycle considered an antique?

- ❑ Is a custom paint job covered automatically under my motorcycle policy?

- ❑ If I change the factory CC size to be higher, will it affect my insurance policy?

- ❑ Will a sidecar add-on affect my motorcycle policy premium?

- ❑ Are motorcycle policies written for less than one year?

- ❑ Is a passenger covered under my motorcycle policy?

- ❑ To purchase motorcycle insurance, do I need a motorcycle license?

Umbrella: Asking the Right Questions?

❑ What liability limits are required on an auto policy to carry an umbrella?

❑ What liability limits are required on a home policy to carry an umbrella?

❑ When will I really need an umbrella policy?

❑ Will it cost more with underage drivers on the umbrella policy?

❑ Will an umbrella policy cost more with more than one vehicle?

❑ What will my total liability limits be if I purchase the umbrella policy?

❑ Do I have liability coverage if I'm on the board of directors for a local business?

❑ Who is covered under my umbrella policy?

❑ What vehicles are covered under my umbrella policy?

❑ What payment options are available if I purchase the umbrella policy?

❑ Will my umbrella policy cover my boat?

❑ Will my umbrella policy cover my rental properties?

❑ Can I have an umbrella policy without an auto insurance policy?

❑ Does my umbrella policy cover my home?

❑ Does my umbrella policy cover me if my dog bites someone?

❑ Can I have an umbrella policy with another insurance carrier?

❑ What deductible do I have on my umbrella policy?

❑ Do I pay higher rates when I have a dog?

❑ Are there dogs the insurance company specifically won't insure under the umbrella policy?

❑ Will trampolines be covered under my umbrella policy?

❑ Will swimming pools be covered under my umbrella policy?

❑ Will my motorcycle be covered under my umbrella policy?

❑ Will my umbrella policy extend to my homeowners policy?

❑ Will being on a board of directors affect my umbrella policy coverage in any way?

❑ What are the limits required by the insurance company to purchase an umbrella policy?

❑ Is an umbrella policy also called excess liability coverage?

Claims:

Asking the Right Questions?

❑ How many estimates should I get after an accident?

❑ Can I keep my vehicle if the insurance company totals it?

❑ Should I go to a chiropractor after an accident?

❑ What types of parts will be used on my vehicle (new, used, remanufactured)?

❑ Will a claims adjuster always look at my car after an accident?

❑ Is damage from an explosion covered under the homeowners policy?

❑ If I hit something lying in the road and damage my tire, do I have coverage?

❑ What things will you need if my car is totaled?

❑ If my car catches fire and is declared a total loss, do I have coverage?

❑ How many days after an accident will elapse before I get called by an adjuster?

❑ Will new parts be used on my wrecked vehicle?

❑ Does insurance cover wind damage to shingles?

❑ Is fire damage a covered loss under comprehensive coverage?

❑ Is glass breakage a covered loss under comprehensive coverage?

❑ Is hail damage a covered loss under comprehensive coverage?

❑ Is theft a covered loss under comprehensive coverage?

❑ Is water damage a covered loss under comprehensive coverage?

❑ If I'm in the middle of a multi-vehicle accident, how should the claim be handled?

❑ When I'm out of state and have an accident, which claims office will be settling my claim?

❑ When hit by someone without insurance, if I have liability only, what are my options?

❑ At what point will the insurance company declare a car to be a total loss?

❑ How are road hazards covered or not covered under my auto policy?

❑ Do I need the police report from an accident?

❑ Should I call the police every time I have an accident or just on certain accidents?

❑ Will my tree falling on my neighbor's house be my insurance company's responsibility or theirs?

❑ If my roof is being replaced from hail damage and I have a replacement coverage policy, do I get the full amount up-front?

❑ When can I expect a check for the depreciation holdback on my roof?

❑ When a tornado sends my house and all my belongings to the next county, how long before I get paid?

❑ What is the maximum dollar amount I will get from my insurance policy today if I had a total property loss claim?

❑ If I have a total fire loss to my house and an insured vehicle is in the garage, will I have two claims or one?

❑ If I have a total fire loss to my house and a car is in the garage, will I have two deductibles or one?

❑ If my motorcycle is totaled, can I buy it back?

❑ Is ice damming covered under my homeowners policy?

❑ If while I am on vacation my vehicle breaks down and I need to stay in a hotel, do I have coverage?

❑ If my clothes and my suitcase are stolen out of my vehicle, are they covered?

❑ If some important books are stolen out of my vehicle, is there coverage for them?

❑ If a windstorm comes through and causes a power outage to my house, do I have coverage for spoiled food?

❑ If lighting strikes the transformer down the street and my electricity goes out, am I covered for damages it causes?

❑ If money is stolen out of my vehicle, do I have coverage?

❑ If money is stolen out of my home do I have coverage?

❑ If my son throws a baseball through my neighbor's window, is my insurance company responsible?

❑ If a paper carrier delivering papers on my property falls and cracks a rib, do I have coverage?

❑ If I have a fire in my apartment, am I responsible for damages to others' apartments?

❑ If an uninsured driver hits me, what options do I have?

❑ Do states have financial responsibility laws to make people pay for damages they cause?

❑ If someone steals my vehicle and injures someone, am I responsible?

❑ If a tree limb falls and cracks the concrete patio foundation, am I covered?

- ❑ If someone falls in my pool while I'm away from home, am I responsible?

- ❑ If trees are down in my backyard from wind, will insurance cover the removal?

- ❑ If lighting strikes the house, do I have coverage?

- ❑ If an animal damages the inside of my house, is it covered?

- ❑ I have water damage in my house from a faulty pipe, is it covered?

- ❑ How many days should I expect to pass before my claim is settled?

- ❑ If my car is keyed in the parking lot at work, will I have to pay a deductible?

- ❑ Explain depreciation and how you calculated it for my claim.

- ❑ After an accident, does my policy guarantee quality repairs?

- ❑ Who is responsible for making sure repairs are done properly?

- ❑ Who is responsible for making sure repairs are done in a timely manor?

- ❑ If my car is totaled, will my insurance company want the title?

- ❑ If a tree falls on an electrical wire attached to my house and does damage to my house, am I covered?

- ❑ Do I have personal property coverage while I'm traveling?

- ❑ Do I have personal property coverage while traveling abroad?

- ❑ Can I use any brand of paint to fix the damages caused by a fire?

- ❑ If the walls in my house are drywall before a claim, is that what they have to be after the claim?

❑ Is a broken or cracked sidewalk ever covered under my homeowners policy?

❑ Is there a guarantee on repair work done to my car?

❑ Is there a guarantee on repair work done to my home?

❑ Is there a guarantee on repair work done to my motorcycle?

❑ How many repair estimates should I get for my home repairs?

❑ How many repair estimates should I get for my auto repairs?

❑ How many repair estimates should I get for my motorcycle repairs?

❑ Will there ever be time when depreciation is not held back?

❑ If the rental coverage is $20 dollars per day up to $600 dollars, will I get the full thirty days of use?

❑ If my computer is sitting on the roof of my car when I begin to move and falls and breaks, is it covered?

❑ Explain what cause of loss means

❑ Explain what moral hazard means.

❑ Is my insurance company responsible to put me back to where I was one second before the accident or loss?

❑ Will my claim be coded on the computer system as a not-at-fault, catastrophic, at-fault, weather, or non–weather-related claim?

Possible Auto Claims	Possible Home Claims
Deer	Ice damming
Hail	Hail
Road hazard	High wind damage
High wind damage	Earthquake
Theft	Fire
Vandalism	Water
Water	Vandalism
Flood	Flood
Head-on collisions	Liability injury
Rock chips	Medical injury
Liability injury	Storm- related
Medical injury	Electrical power surges
Flat tire on the highway	Theft
Rental car needed after accident	Loss of use
Lost income	Money stolen
Fire	Sump pump fails
Storm-related	Sewer backup damage
Crash-related	Tornado damage
Tornado damage	Hurricane damage
Hurricane damage	Pipe in basement breaks
Rock chips	Dog bites
Parking lot accidents	Screens doors blow off from storm
Hit and run parking lot accidents	Lighting strikes
Tree falls on car due to wind storm	Tree falls on covered property
Disability injuries	Jewelry stolen
Custom paint job damaged in accident	Jewelry lost
Glass breakage	Memorable collections lost or stolen

Keys locked in car	Smoke-related
Chain-reaction stoplight accidents	Drive through the garage door
Car broke down, needs to be towed	Guest injured on your property
Friend injured while a passenger	Additional living expenses
Trailer comes unhooked, hits car	Musical instruments at school
Pedestrian hit by your car	House sinks into underground mine
Every loss has to have a cause of loss	**Every loss has to have a cause of loss**

Flood:

Asking

the Right

Question?

❑ Do I need a flood policy?

❑ How do you find out if my home or business is in a flood plain?

❑ What deductibles are available on a flood policy?

❑ What limits should I carry on a flood policy?

❑ Can I carry personal property contents coverage on a flood policy?

❑ Can I insure my property at whatever limit I want?

❑ Explain what an elevation certificate is.

❑ Do I need an elevation certificate?

❑ Will an elevation certificate cost me a fee?

❑ Are there preferred rates for flood polices that are less expensive?

❑ Is there a waiting period before my policy goes into effect?

❑ Will a detached structure on my property need a separate policy?

❑ Whom should I contact if I have flood damage?

❑ Are coverages the same on a flood policy as on my homeowners policy?

❑ Can I make payments on a flood policy?

❑ Is mold covered under a flood policy?

❑ If I cancel my flood policy, will I get a prorated or short-rate refund?

❑ Is there an exception to the thirty-day wait rule for a flood policy?

❑ Is there coverage for the house foundation?

- ❑ If my house is swept away and does damage to other property, am I covered?

- ❑ Will my flood policy ever be cancelled?

- ❑ Can I buy a flood policy even if I'm not in a flood plain?

- ❑ Can I carry whatever limits I want on my flood policy?

- ❑ Is there a maximum amount of coverage that is allowed on a flood policy?

- ❑ Is there a minimum amount of coverage that is allowed on a flood policy?

- ❑ Will flood claim checks be made out to the insured and the mortgage company or just to the insured?

- ❑ How many days will elapse before the claims adjuster will be out and assess the damage after a claim is reported?

- ❑ Does a flood policy have any medical coverage available for the insured?

- ❑ Does a flood policy have any medical coverage for a guest?

- ❑ Will policy claims be settled at replacement cost or actual cash value (ACV)?

- ❑ What is the maximum deductible allowed?

- ❑ What is the minimum deductible allowed?

- ❑ Can I purchase a flood policy for contents only if I'm a renter?

- ❑ Is my auto covered for flood damage?

Split Limit Liability Coverage

Bodily Injury	Bodily Injury	Property Damage
Per Person	Per Accident	Per Accident
20,000	40,000	15,000
25,000	50,000	25,000
50,000	100,000	50,000
100,000	**300,000**	**100,000**
250,000	**500,000**	**100,000**
500,000	1,000,000	500,000

❑ **FYI:**
Liability limits are all found on what is called the **declarations** page.

❑ **FYI:**
Bodily Injury is sometimes referred to as or abbreviated as (BI).

❑ **FYI:**
Property Damage is sometimes referred to as or abbreviated as (PD).

❑ **FYI:**
Most companies require policy limits of either 100,000/ 300,000/ 100,000 or 250,000/ 500,000/ 100,000 to carry an umbrella.

❑ **FYI:**
Typically, a coverage limit of 20,000 / 40,000 / 15,000 is the state minimum across the states.

❑ **FYI:**
Purchase bodily injury liability coverage to cover bodily injury of the other driver and passengers in the event of an accident.

❑ **<u>FYI</u>:**

Purchase property damage liability coverage to cover the other parties' personal property in the event of an accident you cause.

❑ **<u>FYI</u>:**

The insurance always travels with the car.

❑ **<u>FYI</u>:**

Typically, the higher the liability limits, the higher the premium costs.

Medical Expense Coverage / Personal Injury Protection

Medical Expense Coverage limits	Personal Injury Protection limits	
1,000 Minimum	1,000 Minimum	
2,000		
5,000		
10,000		
25,000		
50,000	↓	
100,000	250,000	

❑ **FYI:**
Typically state laws require a minimum coverage to be carried on auto policy.

❑ **FYI:**
Medical expense coverage is for medical injuries to the named insured, as well as passengers in your auto in the event of an accident.

❑ **FYI:**
Loss of income is sometimes included in your medical expense coverage or personal injury protection coverage.

❑ **FYI:**
First dollar medical coverage (pays first) and is typically used together with an Individual's group health or individual health plan.

❑ **FYI:**
Limits will vary from state to state and company to company.

❑ **FYI:**
Personal injury states typically have higher medical limits available.

❑ **FYI:**

Personal injury protection is required coverage by state insurance laws.

❑ **FYI:**

Medical expense coverage is required coverage by state insurance laws.

❑ **FYI:**

Medical expense coverage and personal injury protection do not have a deductible or co-pay that apply.

Uninsured and Underinsured Motorist Bodily Injury Coverage

Uninsured Motorist Coverage	Underinsured Motorist Coverage
20,000 / 40,000	20,000 / 40,000
25,000 / 50,000	25,000 /50,000
50,000 / 100,000	50,000 / 100,000
100,000 / 300,000	100,000 / 300,000
250,000 / 500,000	250,000 / 500,000
500,000 / 1,000,000	500,000 / 1,000,000

Uninsured Motorist Property Damage Coverage
15,000 coverage and 250 deductible

*This coverage, available in certain states, is available for the insured who have liability only cars.

❏ **FYI:**
Another name for uninsured motorist coverage (UM)

❏ **FYI:**
Another name for underinsured motorist coverage (UIM)

❏ **FYI:**
Uninsured motorist coverage and underinsured motorist coverage is for bodily injuries in the event someone that is uninsured or underinsured hits you.

❏ **FYI:**
Uninsured motorist coverage and underinsured motorist coverage can be declined (a form has to be signed).

❑ **FYI:**

You can choose the limits of coverage; they do not have to match the liability limits on the policy.

❑ **FYI:**

Certain states offer uninsured motorist property damage coverage in the event you are hit by an uninsured driver and you carry only liability coverage on your vehicle.

❑ **FYI:**

Uninsured motorist coverage and underinsured motorist coverage limits you carry are consistently the same.

Full Coverage Auto Policy

Comprehensive	Collision	Rental Car	Towing	Loss Of Income
0	0	10 / 300	25	
25	25	15 / 450	50	varies from Company to Company and Coverage
50	50	20 / 600	75	
100	100	25 / 750	100	
250	250	30 / 900		
500	500	40 / 1,200		
1,000	1,000	50 / 1,500		

Additional Coverage
death and disability available

❑ **FYI:**
Comprehensive coverage is sometimes referred to as "Other than Collision)."

❑ **FYI:**
Comprehensive coverage examples include hail damage, hit deer, theft, vandalism, fire damage, and glass breakage.

❑ **FYI:**
Comprehensive coverage carried by itself is typically referred to as storage coverage. A vehicle is stored and not driven for a period of time.

❑ **FYI:**
Comprehensive coverage can be carried without collision and is subject to a deductible of your choosing.

❑ **<u>FYI:</u>**

Typically, collision coverage is carried with comprehensive coverage, not by itself.

❑ **<u>FYI:</u>**

Collision coverage covers damage to your vehicles and is subject to a deductible of your choosing.

❑ **<u>FYI:</u>**

Rental coverage is subject to a per-day limit when vehicle is in a body shop.

❑ **<u>FYI:</u>**

Typically, towing is included in roadside assistant coverage.

Discounts

Possible Auto Discounts	Possible Home Discounts
Multi-car	Auto Home
Multi-policy	Security System
Air Bag	Dead Bolts
Safe Car	Smoke Detectors
Non-smoker	Non-smoker
Non-drinker	Claim Free
Anti-theft	Paperless
Good Student	Fire Extinguisher
Low Miles Driven	High Deductibles
Empty Nest	Profession
Away School	Multi-policy
Claim-free	Senior Discount
Accident- and Ticket-free	Empty Nest
Paid in Full	Paid in Full
Paperless	New Roof
High Deductible	Distance from Fire Station
Profession	Distance from Fire Hydrant
Auto Home	Suburban Fire Rating
Safe Driver	Monthly Electronic Billing
Anti-lock Brakes	Safety Devices

❑ **FYI:**

there may be some variations to the above discounts mentioned.

❑ **FYI:**

Discounts save money; take advantage of them by asking about the availability.

❑ **FYI:**

Discounts can apply to certain vehicles and not others.

❑ **FYI:**

Discounts can have percentages attached to them. Beware: for example, with multi-car discounts, the higher number of cars the higher percentage of discount.

❑ **FYI:**

One of the first questions asked should be what discounts apply to my policy.

❑ **FYI:**

Discounts will vary from company to company.

❑ **FYI:**

New and different discounts are continually being changed or updated.

Four-car Chain Reaction Accident

❑ **FYI:**
Stay calm and call the police.

❑ **FYI:**
Make sure you're looking for witnesses and get their names, phone numbers, and addresses.

❑ **FYI:**
You need to understand your insurance company might have to take care of your damages at first until fault is determined.

❑ **FYI:**
Insurance companies are not going to do anything until they have recorded statements and know who was at fault.

❑ **FYI:**
If your car is not drivable and has to be towed, you need to understand that the storage company charges you by the day for storing your car.

❑ **FYI:**
Depending on the state in which you live, the requirement for sending in the accident report to the state may vary from just a few days from the accident date to couple of weeks.

❑ **FYI:**
Each insurance company might settle the claim for their insured then subrogate to the at-fault insurance company.

❑ **FYI:**
If your car only has liability, you may have to wait for the at-fault insurance company to pay your damages after fault is determined, and this may take a few days.

Parking Lot Accident

❏ **FYI:**
When you're leaving the parking lot, be sure you are aware of your surroundings. Make sure you have glanced around to see if anyone is in his or her car.

❏ **FYI:**
Look for taillights being on and especially backup lights.

❏ **FYI:**
The insurance companies are going take recorded statements from both of the insureds.

❏ **FYI:**
The insurance companies might rule that each is a percentage at-fault, maybe a 50% / 50% split, a 60% / 40% split, or even a different percentage split.

❏ **FYI:**
The police usually don't get involved much if you have a parking lot accident. They may come out, but that is about it.

❏ **FYI:**
Witnesses are very important with parking lot accidents so as you're getting out of your car be sure to glance around to see if anyone is walking around that might have seen something.

❏ **FYI:**
Be sure that you make your insurance company aware that this was not your fault and that it should not go against your record. Be persistent.

❏ **FYI:**
Make sure that you get the other person's name and phone number and a correct address before leaving the scene of the accident.

❏ **FYI:**
Remember, the small fender bender in the parking lot is just as bad as a big accident.

Hypothetical Situations

Examples of Very Real Possibilities
with
Thought-provoking Detail
and
Eye-opening Reality

Need To Ask Questions

As you are reading through the hypothetical situation section you may recall or have variations of similar situations. You may also begin to ask yourself *Could this happen to me?*, or in some cases it might bring back some memories. Ask yourself as you're reading through what things could have happened or not happened to prevent the outcomes. All of these situations create potential insurance claims. With claims come potential problems—for example injuries, damaged property, cancelled policies, lawsuits, frustration, higher insurance rates, and many others.

Hypothetical situations sometime seem to appear trivial, funny, or unbelievable. However, to trivialize any of the hypothetical situations is like making statements that you are 100 percent certain nothing like these will ever happen. Use these hypothetical situations to your advantage; think of them as tools you have in your insurance knowledge tool chest. As a carpenter always says, you can do anything with the right tools.

Because insurance is an intangible product, the more knowledge you have and the better informed you are, the better off and easier your potential decisions might be. As the determined runner preparing for marathons seeks every advantage he or she can find for his or her running tool chest, so you too should seek every advantage for your insurance knowledge tool chest.

A tool chest full of carpenter tools can create opportunities for carpenters beyond their belief. It can allow them to use their imaginations to create, form, and build. Likewise, having your insurance knowledge tool chest full has the potential to create confidence and understanding that can be used in ways beyond your belief. While you are reading, imagine you were right there when the hypothetical situation happened.

❑ I left late for work on Monday morning. I was speeding down the street five blocks from my house, thinking only of the consequences of being late again. I stopped at the first stop sign but ran the next stop sign down the street. In a matter of seconds, two families had their lives changed.

❑ I was coming home late one night. I was tired from a long day's drive. As I approached a curve, I dozed off and went airborne. I eventually stopped, but not before my car was damaged and a farmhouse was damaged.

❑ I was backing out of my stall at the grocery store. I was in a hurry and forgot to look as I was backing. To my surprise, a car across the lane was backing out the same time, and we hit in the middle. Both cars had damage in the rear of the car.

❑ My wife and I pulled into my parking spot at the mall with our brand new vehicle. We went in the mall for less than fifteen minutes, came out, and we had a dent on the drivers side door. To our disbelief, there was no note letting us know who did it or what happened.

❑ My wife and I just got married several months ago. She, being the athletic type, joined a running club just weeks after we were married. Last Friday I said good-bye and have a great run. With a smile on her face she ran out the door for a three-mile run. Twenty-three minutes later when she returned, the smile was gone—and not because she was tired. She'd lost the diamond out of her $2000 ring.

❑ Last summer our family moved to an acreage with ten acres of pasture land. Our oldest daughter loves horses, so we decided to purchase one for her to take care of. On a stormy night a few weeks after getting the horse, the door blew off its hinges, and as a result our daughter's horse got out and ran in front of a passing car. The driver took evasive action to miss the horse and ended up in the ditch upside down.

❑ Last night a severe thunderstorm came through the area where I live. I woke up to a noise or crash of some sort coming from the backyard. However, because of it being 2:00 AM and dark and still raining, I couldn't go outside, so I went back to bed. The next morning I looked outside; to my amazement the forty-foot oak tree in my neighbors' yard was lying on my fence.

❑ The night of July 3rd a serve thunderstorm came through the area, dropping five inches of rain overnight. When I woke the next morning I looked outside, and things seemed fine. So I carried on with my business of getting ready for the day. When I walked downstairs to take the dog out I noticed the basement floor was wet with several inches of water at one end of the basement. As I examined the area where the water was, I noticed a wet spot on the wall. Water was coming from the outside and seeping through the walls.

❑ The 1973 Chevrolet SS that I just restored has been insured on a personal auto policy. I decided to take it out for a Saturday night drive last weekend for the first time since restoring it. I was so proud of that car. However, as I was returning home around ten o'clock, I saw something out of the corner of my eye. As I got closer I realized a deer was coming up out of the ditch without any time to react. Thud! I get out, ready to cry, and see a deer lying on ground in front of the car. I then glance at the front of my car, hoping for the best. Unfortunately, all I could see were mangled parts, steaming engine, and anti-freeze on the ground.

❑ My daughter's music teacher asked her to bring her violin in for a tuning up before orchestra starts next Thursday. As she was running out the door to catch the school bus I yelled to her to be careful with the violin. Unfortunately, I spoke too late. I watched it skid along the ground and come to a rest at the curb with the violin lying on the ground, scratched, and broken strings flipping everywhere, along with a broken case with scuff marks.

❑ My family was on vacation. While we were stopped at a traffic light, a speeding motorist hit our car from behind. I jumped out to make sure all parties where okay then called the local police and fire department to the accident scene. Shortly after making the call I heard the police coming. The responding police officer took my driver's license, insurance information, and car registration information and made out his report. He then gave me a copy of the report, and as I was reading it over I noticed that the driver who hit me had no insurance.

❑ I was hit in the driver's door, and glass shattered everywhere. Fortunately, the only injuries I received were a few cuts from the flying glass.

❑ I was stopped at an intersection with a red light. A speeding vehicle came up from behind and hit me from behind. The impact caused whiplash, and my wife and I had to be seen by a chiropractor.

❑ I was traveling at night out on the open highway. Suddenly, I heard this funny noise at the front of the car. I began to focus my attention on the gauges in my car. The gauge with numbers began to creep up, and then I began to hear a whistle. I pulled off the road and got out. As I lifted the hood, steam came rolling out like a ball of fire. Just as I'd thought, I'd lost a fan belt and my car started to overheat.

❑ As I rushed out the door with my car keys in one hand and my laptop computer in the other, I stumbled and dropped the keys under my car. So I set my computer on the roof of my car and got down on one knee to grab my keys. With only one thing on my mind—getting to the airport—I jumped in the car and rushed off. A few blocks down the street I heard a noise. I glanced over toward the passenger seat where I always set my laptop computer. I then realized what I had heard.

❑ My insurance payment was due on Friday, and my insurance policy was due to cancel if not paid. As I was leaving to go to work I turned to my wife and said the car insurance is due. She thought I'd sent it in, and I thought she'd sent it in. That night, leaving work and as usual in a hurry to start the weekend, I took my foot off the brake and barely tapped the car in front me. When my wife and I got home and shared our day, the first thing we asked each other was did we send in the insurance payment. To our chagrin, neither one of us had sent the payment in. What more could go wrong, I said as the phone rang. To my surprise the person I'd hit was already calling with an estimate of $2500.

❑ A rash of burglaries in our neighborhood had given us cause for concern. My sister's daughter invited my wife and me to her high school graduation. We decided that it was very important for us to be there for her at this special time of her life. We were gone for two days and two nights and had lots of fun with my niece. We said good-bye, packed up, and headed for home. As we pulled into the driveway I could see something that looked different than when we left. The city garbage container was knocked over. I asked my wife if she had bumped it as we were leaving. When she said no, I knew something was wrong. I decided immediately that I should call the police for safety reasons.

❏ An F-3 tornado packing strong winds came through our town last night. Trees and power lines were down all over town. The city was declared a disaster area. In my yard alone I had two trees that fell not hitting anything and one that toppled over onto my garage. The garage had extensive damage with a hole at the peak.

❏ I was so excited when I realized my motorcycle had sold on eBay yesterday. I made arrangements to have it picked up over the weekend. When the people picked it up they paid me in cash. No banks were open, so the money sat on my desk for two days. Monday morning I realized I had to get the money to the bank. Unfortunately, it was gone from my desk and nowhere to be found.

❏ As the storm was passing through, it was like the floodgates had opened up. The streets were flooded, and city sewers were overflowing like an Old Faithful geyser. The electricity suddenly went off as the storm continued to intensify. Once the electricity went off, I knew problems lay ahead. I went down to the basement to check on the sump pump. As I opened the basement door, I knew we had problems; there was water standing near the drain and the carpet was already wet in the family room next to the laundry room.

❏ My wife and I received that dreaded call a parent never wants to get that their child was in an accident. I didn't know all the details. I just knew that it might be bad. When I walked into the emergency room, my heart was pounding like I had just run a marathon. I anxiously asked the nurse where my daughter was and could I see her. The nurse gave me as much information as she knew: that my daughter was stable, awake, and had serious injuries. Several families were impacted by this one car accident.

❑ On my way home from work last night I was following a semi. I was approximately two car lengths away from the back of the truck. To my surprise, shortly before I was to exit off the road it seemed to start hailing. The fact of the matter was the semi had picked up some loose gravel and sprayed it all over my car. I continued my journey home from a long day at work, and as I was pulling into my drive the reflection from my yard light off my windshield magnified a crack just above the passenger side windshield wiper.

❑ The ice storm that hit our area made traveling very treacherous. I had only fifty miles to go before I was safely home. I was anxious to get home and very tired from the long trip. As I was coming upon some slower traffic, I slowed down to a modest speed when suddenly my car takes off in a tailspin. I had just become a victim of the hazards of winter driving and black ice on a bridge.

❑ The grandson was over at our house playing near the backyard swing set. While playing he slipped and fell against the ladder attached to the swing set fort. He did not seem to have broken anything, but to be safe I suggested that he be seen by a doctor. The emergency room doctor diagnosed a fracture.

❑ My day seemed to be going just fine until I got behind the wheel of the family car. With my mind focused on getting to an appointment and not focused on driving, I accidentally put the car into R for reverse and accelerated. To my amazement, rather then traveling down the driveway and onto the street I ended up backing into our garage door.

❑ The storm front that came through packed a big punch. A lighting strike seemed to hit every couple minutes. The storm sirens for our city were blaring. After a long period of calm the storm seemed to fire up again. Suddenly, I heard a loud boom and a crash; the lights went out, and it appeared everything had just gone completely dead. For the next twenty-four hours candlelight was all we had. The next morning I was up early surveying the damage. The large tree in the backyard had been struck by lighting. The power lines coming into the house were being stretched to their limits with tree branches. It appeared as though a mini tornado had come through.

☐ Last Friday I called the auto body shop to see when our car was going to be done and ready to be picked up. They told me it was going to be couple of days. Thankfully, I still had the rental and was able to use it for travel back and forth to work. However, parking the rental car in the parking lot didn't protect it from the hazards around it. When I took the car back it had scratches on the passenger side rear fender and on the bumper. As the rental agent was inspecting the vehicle for damages they asked me if I knew how these scratches happened. The only thing I could say was it happened in the work parking lot. To my displeasure, upon reviewing my purchase contract, I realized I had declined any coverages the rental agency had offered.

☐ Last night one inch of freezing rain and five inches of snow covered the ground and everything exposed. This was a very odd storm that came through because it came days before the first day of spring. The clean, white snow was beautiful. However, in a few days the temperature started to become more seasonal and normal. I was glad to see warmer temperatures. What I wasn't glad to see was the water stains on my living room ceiling. This was something new I just discovered since the snow started melting. It appeared my roof was leaking.

☐ The last few weeks have been busy at work. So to get caught up I started working at home and nights after work. My laptop computer was sitting on my desk in the family room. The dog was running around house barking because the neighbor who was walking his dog had just gone by on the sidewalk. Realizing the front door was open I quickly jumped to my feet and ran to shut the door. However, what I didn't realize was the electrical cord to my laptop computer had somehow gotten caught on my chair. And as I got up and pushed the chair back, the force of pushing the chair back also caused a simultaneous crash of my computer on the floor. To my amazement and displeasure, the tool I use most for my work was now nothing more than broken pieces lying all over the floor of the family room.

☐ Typically Sparky is our loveable pet dog. He wouldn't hurt anyone. However, last Saturday, when the neighbor stopped by to say hi, Sparky seemed to be acting somewhat defensively, and he barked and growled. Confidently, our neighbor reached out to pet Sparky. As he did that Sparky seemed to come alive like an attack dog. I was unable to get between Sparky and the neighbor to ward off an attack; the neighbor's hand became lunch for our family pet. Thankfully, Sparky only broke the skin with his teeth, and nothing was broken.

❑ I usually drive the car in the garage on Friday night after I wash it. I seem to be a creature of habit. However, on this one Friday in May I decided to leave the car parked in the driveway. As we were getting ready to go to my mom and dad's house for Mother's day the phone rang. A deep voice on the other end asked me if I owned a silver Honda Civic. I said yes. He responded by saying I needed to come and identify it at the police station.

Glossary

- ❑ **(ACV) Actual Cash Value** – cost of replacing damaged or destroyed property with comparable new property, minus depreciation and obsolescence.

- ❑ **All Risk Policy** – basically, if it is not listed as an exclusion in the policy, then there is coverage.

- ❑ **Arbitration** – non-interested third party is assigned to decide fault in an accident.

- ❑ **Betterment** – an improvement or improvements made on insured property that increases the value.

- ❑ **Clue Report** – report used by the insurance company that shows the history of accidents and claims paid out for a client or potential client.

- ❑ **Coinsurance** – in property insurance, requires the policyholder to carry insurance equal to a specified percentage of the value of the property to receive full payment on a loss.

- ❑ **Comprehensive Coverage** – pays for damage to or the loss of your vehicle from causes other then collisions (examples are deer and hail).

- ❑ **Collision Coverage** – covers physical damage to your vehicle.

- ❑ **Credit Score** – insurance companies use credit scoring to determine your insurance premium.

❑ **Depreciation** – decrease in the value of property over time due to use or wear or tear.

❑ **Declarations Page** – the page in the policy that shows the names and addresses, periods of time a policy is in force, the premium, and coverage.

❑ **Earned Premium** – the amount of the premium that has been paid for in advance that has been "earned" by virtue of the fact that time has passed. .

❑ **Exclusion** – a provision in the policy that denies coverage for perils, people, or locations.

❑ **Frequency** – insurance companies look closely at the number of claims a client might have in a period of time.

❑ **Gap Insurance** – insurance that pays the difference between the actual cash value of a vehicle and the amount still to be paid on the loan.

❑ **Hazard** – a circumstance that increases the likelihood or probable severity of loss.

❑ **Insurance** – a contract purchased to guarantee compensation for a covered loss.

❑ **Liability Insurance** – insurance that pays and renders service on behalf of an insured for a loss arising out his or her responsibility, due to negligence, to others imposed by law, or assumed by contract.

❑ **Loss of Use** – another name for additional living expense (ALE) insurance policies that reimburse policyholders for living expense to live somewhere while their home is being restored.

❑ **Medical Expense Insurance** – pays limited medical and funeral expenses if the policyholder, family member, or passenger in the car is injured or killed.

- **Non-owner Policy** – auto insurance coverage that offers liability, uninsured motorist, and medical payments to a named insured who does not own a vehicle.

- **Named Peril Policy** –- perils specifically covered on insured property.

- **Obsolescence** – decrease in the value of property as a result of technological advancement and changing social mores.

- **Peril** – the cause of a possible loss.

- **Personal Injury Protection Insurance** – pays basic expenses for an insured and his or her family in states with no-fault auto insurance.

- **Pro Rata** – insurance policy cancellation refund.

- **Property Damage Coverage** – physical damage to property.

- **Replacement Cost** – insurance coverage that pays the dollar amount needed to replace the structure or personal property without deducting for depreciation but limited by the policy limits.

- **Severity** – insurance companies look closely at the total degree of claims.

- **Subrogation** – the circumstance where an insurance company takes the place of an insured to pursue remedies against a third party.

- **(VIN) Vehicle identification Number** – Seventeen-digit number that identifies the insured vehicle. Usually stamped on vehicle title, registration, and/or dashboard of vehicle.

Answer Log

Answer To Questions Asked	Company and Person Answering Question	Day and Time Answered

Key Insurance Words

Across:

1 - A clause in an insurance policy that makes a claim jointly payable to the policyholder and the party who holds the mortgage

3 - Hit a deer

4 - The part of the premium applicable to the unexpired part of the policy period

5 - Six months

7 - The right of an insurer who has taken over another's loss, you give up your right to pursue settlement

12 - Claim pay out was large

17 - Covers physical damage to the insured's automobile

20 - The practice of appraising and controlling risk

21 - Perils specifically covered on insured

Down:

2 - Section of the policy that lists whats not covered

6 - listed at the top of the dec page

8 - Blanket coverage

9 - The dollar amount needed to replace damaged personal property or dwelling property without deducting for depreciation

10 - Equitable transfer of the risk of a loss from one entity to another in exchange for payment

11 - Who, what, where, when, why, how much

13 - Coverage if an insured is legally liable for bodily injury

14 - A policy condition that enables an insured to direct the company to pay any loss to a third party

15 - Money held back until repairs are finished

property
24 - List of damages
25 - A circumstance that increases the likelihood or probable severity of loss
26 - Saves money on your policy
27 - Coverage if an insured is legally liable for property damage
29 - Cancelled because of to many claims
30 - Cost of replacing damaged or destroyed property with comparable new property,minus depreciation and obsolescence.
31 - When damage to vehicle is more then the car is worth
32 - Insurance for motorist who have been canceled or refused insurance
34 - Covers an insured who is hit by a driver who has no liability insurance
36 - The amount of premium that has been paid for in advance and used
37 - The agreed amount for six months or a year
38 - How premiums are determined
39 - Proof of insurance sent to the bank or mortgage company
40 - 0, 50,100, 200, 500,1000 amount of loss before insurance pays

16 - Notice sent out to insured
18 - The dollar amount associated with a claim
19 - A demand made by the insured
22 - Tickets and accidents are on this report
23 - Something carried in wallet or purse
28 - Monthly payment method
33 - Wind, Hail, lighting, tornado
34 - Abbreviation of uninsured motorist coverage
35 - Abbreviation of underinsured motorist coverage

Possible Answers:

ACV, Cancellation , Claim, Collision coverage, Comprehensive, Credit score, Declarations, Deductible, Depreciation hold back, Discount, Earned premium, EFT, Estimate, Exclusion, Frequency, Hazard, Identification card, Insurance, Insurance binder, Liability insurance, loss, Loss Payee clause, Mortgage Clause , MVR, Named insured, Named perils, Nonstandard auto, Perils, Policy Period, Premium, Property damage, Replacement cost, Risk Management, Severity, Subrogation, Totaled, UIM, UM, Umbrella, Unearned premium, Uninsured Motorist Coverage

100 Important Insurance Words

```
U T T F I W L A E Y D M E U K N E B X Y Z S S M M D N P Z G X G
J W Q R F P X A C V T X K U F Q Q R K T U N M P R Q U O D O M L
Y L Y E M E X N F U O P S S U B R O G A T I O N U E A T L U D H
P X O Q L N F V V U M H J D L R I K B S Y D K U L M V R G M Q Q
P E N U D W E M G A O T H H L E B N K K R W E Y A H A F T O L I
S N D E C L A R A T I O N S P A G E V S E T A D P U G K D W D U
H D I N Y H Y C O W B I A U A K N A D Y F W L H P I K L E I Y Q
U O S C P F M Z R M D H B P Y E V B E A T O A S P M E C A I I O
C R T Y B D W E L L I N G F I R E D P W O P R O R A T A U K B F
S S Q U A R E F O O T I T L E B J E R E B A M E E S T R T R Z J
K E B Q M A O E S T I M A T E O W D E A Y Y H N M U Q N H R R C
H M T S F E X Q S G T E X V X X N U C I C R E D I T S C O R E H
S E V J C U S T O M I Z A T I O N C I R S T A N U H H A R E N W
K N N I F W I W F X Y S N U E H J T A B L O I C M G B N I N T R
O T Y C N Q D D I S C O U N T S U I T A Z W N D D V K C Z T A G
O S S U O F A X N O E H S K Y O T B I G Y I L R E Y S E A E L Y
B T O M N M O U C X R C L A I M C L O P H N A I A R O L T R C H
E O M B R I P R O T Y Q N D L B V E N X T G N V D E C L I S O D
U R G R E E N R M E D I C A L E X P E N S E D E B P I A O P V H
L A X E N W F S E A B S P R R E D I R J U L M R O L A T N O E H
B G W L E A U U U H T I H A H U Z W P L C E A S L A L I F L R H
Y E P L W I M Y N R E I N O P Y S J T R F C R L T C S O O I A G
L C G A A V O E L D E N O D R E U N V O G T I I S E E N R C G E
L O A P L E N K D R O D S N E T R A I O T R N C U M C O M Y E G
E V K O A R T A L P E N P I B R R L Y D J I E E T E U T A U T A
K E E L P F H I M C E T S L V U N A E G R C T N D N R F R C A M
L R A I S O L O C E E R R I U E R E T S J A Y S D T I A B K D A
V A T C E R Y I M K D R I A X M M E G E S L Z E H C T U I K E D
Y G F Y C M E I A E E I T L U M B Z A R Y O O A D O Y L T V V Y
E E A E O I O I G B D T N I H Q O I S U A K Y S H S S T R N I T
T O U A L N D D N N I C S S F Y P N N E H H Q A S T W F A F T R
N U L R L S A E E S I L C E U I A K T G T E C H D K X Q T K C E
Q E T O I U C D N L T D I N V R C P C H U T D E S H O K I C E P
W D O O S R V U A T C A N T B E E A N A P P L I C A T I O N F O
T U T F I A L L R I S K T E Y N R D T W F O D E S I F R N Q F R
Z E A A O N M X Z C A J X E P E V I W E O K L A M S V G I F E P
E W L G N C L U E R E P O R T W T X T S W D Y I T E F R W B B H
P M E E S E X C L U S I O N O A C Z H Y I R F R C E N K E V B K
G R D S D L A D D I T I O N A L C O V E R A G E X Y S T P S O N
A I Y I Q E X V W Y Y G J F I P T N E M R E T T E B U E N T D W
```

ABS	Accidents	ACV
Additional Coverage	AIR Bag	All risk
Application	Arbitration	Atfault
Authorization Form	Auto	Betterment
Binder	Birthday	Breaker Box
Cancellation	Certificate	Claim
Clue Report	Collision	Comprehensive
Credit Card	Credit Score	Customization
Dead Bolts	Declarations page	Deductible
Depreciation	Discounts	Down Pay
Drivers License	Dwelling Fire	Effective Date
EFT	Electrical	Endorsements
Estimate	Exclusion	Frequency
Full Pay	Green	Hazard Insurance
Home	Information Bureau	Inland Marine
Insurance	Kelly Blue Book	Lapse
liability	loss	Loss of Income
Make	Medical Expense	Model
Monthly	MVR	NADA
Named Insured	Named Peril	Nonrenewal
Notfault	Paperless	Pending
Peril	Plumbing updates	Premium
Pro Rata	Property Damage	Quarterly
Refund	Reinstate	Renewal
Rental Coverage	Renters Policy	Replacement Cost
Rider	Roof Age	Service Charge
Settlement	Severity	Short Rate
Six Month Policy	Smoke Alarm	Social Security
Square Foot	Storage Coverage	Subrogation
Tickets	Title	Totaled
Towing	Two Pay	UIM
UM	Umbrella Policy	Uninsured
Updates	VIN	Waiver Form
Year		

100 Important Insurance Words

```
U T T F I W L A E Y D M E U K N E B X Y Z S S M M D N P Z G X G
J W Q R F P X A C V T X K U F Q Q R K T U N M P R Q U O D O M L
Y L Y E M E X N F U O P S S U B R O G A T I O N U E A T L U D H
P X O Q L N F V V U M H J D L R I K B S Y D K U L M V R G M Q Q
P E N U D W E M G A O T H H L E B N K K R W E Y A H A F T O L I
S N D E C L A R A T I O N S P A G E V S E T A D P U G K D W D U
H D I N Y H Y C O W B I A U A K N A D Y F W L H P I K L E I Y Q
U O S C P F M Z R M D H B P Y E V B E A T O A S P M E C A I I O
C R T Y B D W E L L I N G F I R E D P W O P R O R A T A U K B F
S Q U A R E F O O T I T L E B J E R E B A M E E S T R T R Z J
K E B Q M A O E S T I M A T E O W D E A Y Y H N M U Q N H R R C
H M T S F E X Q S G T E X V X X N U C I C R E D I T S C O R E H
S E V J C U S T O M I Z A T I O N C I R S T A N U H H A R E N W
K N N I F W I W F X Y S N U E H J T A B L O I C M G B N I N T R
O T Y C N Q D D I S C O U N T S U I T A Z W N D D V K C Z T A G
O S S U O F A X N O E H S K Y O T B I G Y I L R E Y S E A E L Y
B T O M N M O U C X R C L A I M C L O P H N A I A R O L T R C H
E O M B R I P R O T Y Q N D L B V E N X T G N V D E C L I S O D
U R G R E E N R M E D I C A L E X P E N S E D E B P I A O P V H
L A X E N W F S E A B S P R R E D I R J U L M R O L A T N O E H
B G W L E A U U U H T I H A H U Z W P L C E A S L A L I F L R H
Y E P L W I M Y N R E I N O P Y S J T R F C R L T C S O O I A G
L C G A A V O E L D E N O D R E U N V O G T I I S E E N R C G E
L O A P L E N K D R O D S N E T R A I O T R N C U M C O M Y E G
E V K O A R T A L P E N P I B R R L Y D J I E E T E U T A U T A
K E E L P F H I M C E T S L V U N A E G R C T N D N R F R C A M
L R A I S O L O C E E R R I U E R E T S J A Y S D T I A B K D A
V A T C E R Y I M K D R I A X M M E G E S L Z E H C T U I K E D
Y G F Y C M E I A E E I T L U M B Z A R Y O O A D O Y L T V V Y
E A E O I O I G B D T N I H Q O I S U A K Y S B S S T R N I T R
T O U A L N D D N N I C S S F Y P N N E H H Q A S T W F A F T R
N U L R L S A E E S I L C E U I A K T G T E C H D K X Q T K C E
Q E T O I U C D N L T D I N V R C P C H U T D E S H O K I C E P
W D O O S R V U A T C A N T B E E A N A P P L I C A T I O N F O
T U T F I A L L R I S K T E Y N R D T W F O D E S I F R N Q F R
Z E A A O N M X Z C A J X E P E V I W E O K L A M S V G I F E P
E W L G N C L U E R E P O R T W T X T S W D Y I T E F R W B B H
P M E E S E X C L U S I O N O A C Z H Y I R F R C E N K E V B K
G R D S D L A D D I T I O N A L C O V E R A G E X Y S T P S O N
A I Y I Q E X V W Y Y G J F I P T N E M R E T T E B U E N T D W
```